WHAT A FEW NICE PEOPLE HAD TO SAY...

"Families are accustomed to counting down the days to Christmas. But when it comes to spiritual celebrations for the people of God, Easter tops the list! This powerful, do-able, Bible-driven journey will prepare your hearts to worship the King of Kings and Lord of Lords...the risen Christ!"

Rob Rienow (Pastor, Author, and Founder of *Visionary Family Ministries*)

"I am a firm believer that there is nothing more worthwhile to do with our time on earth than to intimately know Jesus Christ. The *Lent Scripture Journey* draws our hearts to do just that. Keith leads us through Scripture, helping us get a glimpse into the character and person of Jesus. Get to know who He is... and you will come away changed!"

Eva Kubasiak (Host of the *Bible Study Made Simple* Podcast)

"In his book, *Lent Scripture Journey* Keith takes us through an unforgettable quest that is thought-provoking and Jesus-centered. This book will not only challenge you to grow in your faith, but give you a fresh perspective of who Jesus is!"

Chad Owens (Kidmin Coach, Speaker, and Pastor)

"Keith Ferrin has an exciting experience for you...or your entire family. Come discover the true meaning of Lent by journeying with Jesus from the angel's promise to conquering death! Come and worship the Messiah!"

Stanley Mearse (Children's Pastor, Estenalee Baptist Church)

"I love this format for families! Keith has created a devotional that is simple as well as deep. You do not need a large amount of time to do this each day, and you are guaranteed to be challenged in your walk with Jesus. Whether you are a seasoned Christian or new to the faith, you will benefit from this reading and reflection as you walk through this season of Lent."

Christen Clark (Host of the *Collide Kids* Podcast)

"One thing I know about Keith Ferrin is he is passionate about God's Word. I expect that your love for God's Word will increase and grow as you go on this scripture journey for Lent. I believe it will enable the discussions with your family to be meaningful and something you will treasure for years to come. Dive in!"

Yancy (Dove Award-Winning Songwriter, Worship Leader & Author)

"Keith Ferrin's passion for making the Bible relational shines as he invites us to journey with Jesus throughout the season of Lent as individuals, families, and church communities. Simple, impactful, and deep as we look at the life of Jesus as a whole and celebrate Christ our resurrected King!"

Cera Talamantes, Associate Pastor of Family Ministries at Mosaic Church LC

Lent Scripture Journey

Preparing Our Hearts and Minds to Celebrate the Empty Tomb

Keith Ferrin

KF

keithferrin.com

Keith Ferrin Productions, LLC

Copyright © 2022 by Keith Ferrin

Published by Keith Ferrin Productions, LLC

Scripture quotations have been taken from the Christian Standard Bible®, Copyright © 2017 by Holman Bible Publishers. Used by permission. Christian Standard Bible® and CSB® are federally registered trademarks of Holman Bible Publishers.

Back cover photo: Scott Yamamura, Created to Create, Seattle, WA

ISBN: 9798421684268

All rights reserved. Written permission must be secured from the publisher to use or reproduce any part of this book, except for brief quotations in critical reviews or articles.

For information or to schedule author appearances:

Keith Ferrin

www.keithferrin.com

keith@keithferrin.com

Contents

Introduction	X
How to Use This Book	XIII
1. Week 1 – Ash Wednesday	1
2. Week 1 – Thursday	4
3. Week 1 – Friday	7
4. Week 1 – Saturday	10
5. Week 2 – Monday	13
6. Week 2 – Tuesday	16
7. Week 2 – Wednesday	19
8. Week 2 – Thursday	22
9. Week 2 – Friday	25
10. Week 2 – Saturday	28
11. Week 3 – Monday	31
12. Week 3 – Tuesday	34
13. Week 3 – Wednesday	37
14. Week 3 – Thursday	40

15.	Week 3 – Friday	43
16.	Week 3 – Saturday	46
17.	Week 4 – Monday	49
18.	Week 4 – Tuesday	52
19.	Week 4 – Wednesday	55
20.	Week 4 – Thursday	58
21.	Week 4 – Friday	61
22.	Week 4 – Saturday	64
23.	Week 5 – Monday	67
24.	Week 5 – Tuesday	70
25.	Week 5 – Wednesday	73
26.	Week 5 – Thursday	76
27.	Week 5 – Friday	79
28.	Week 5 – Saturday	82
29.	Week 6 – Monday	85
30.	Week 6 – Tuesday	88
31.	Week 6 – Wednesday	91
32.	Week 6 – Thursday	94
33.	Week 6 – Friday	97
34.	Week 6 – Saturday	100
35.	Week 7 – Monday	103
36.	Week 7 – Tuesday	106
37.	Week 7 – Wednesday	109
38.	Week 7 – Thursday	112
39.	Week 7 – Friday	115

40. Week 7 – Saturday	118
41. Easter Sunday	121
About the Author	123
A Few of My Other Books	125
Let's Connect!	128
	130

Introduction

Welcome to the *Lent Scripture Journey*. Many people incorrectly view Lent is as a "Catholic-only" tradition, when in fact, many Protestant Christians have also celebrated Lent throughout history. While there is no *requirement* to celebrate Lent, each individual, family, and church community will most definitely benefit from *preparing our hearts and minds* for a celebration of Christ's resurrection on Easter Sunday!

A simple-and-incredibly-short history of Lent...

Some have thought Lent was established by the apostles in the years following Christ's death, resurrection, and ascension. Officially, nothing was mentioned about Lent until Irenaeus of Lyons (in Western Europe) and Tertullian (in Northern Africa) talked about it in the latter part of the 2nd Century. And here's the kicker: Lent was only 40 *hours*...not 40 *days*!

Dionysius (from Alexandria) stretched that out to six days in the 3rd Century. It wasn't until the Council of Nicea (A.D. 325) that the length was officially locked in at 40 days. The significance of 40 days comes from Jesus fasting and being tempted in the wilderness for 40 days. As a way to participate, honor, and remember Jesus's suffering, many Christians "give something up" for Lent. The idea behind this is that anytime you crave what you've given up, you should give thanks for all that Jesus gave up for you and let that lead you to a time of gratitude, worship, and prayer.

You might notice that from Ash Wednesday through Easter morning is actually 46 days. Most Lent devotionals do not include the six Sundays as part of Lent. For people who choose to include "giving something up" for Lent, many see each Sunday as a mini-resurrection celebration and partake in whatever they have given up. The *Lent Scripture Journey* follows the 40-day reading plan, and therefore, you will not find readings for any of the Sundays.

Also, many Lent devotionals focus only on *Holy Week* (the events from Palm Sunday through Easter Morning). Others look at specific themes of prayer, fasting, generosity, or suffering.

The *Lent Scripture Journey* is going to be a bit different. The "theme" we will explore over the next 40 days is the life of Jesus as a whole. His whole life and purpose pointed to his death and resurrection. Each encounter, teaching, conversation, or miracle pointed to the defeating of death and the restoration of relationship designed to last for all eternity.

That's the journey we are about to go on. A journey through the life of Jesus. A journey toward the cross. A journey toward the empty tomb. And ultimately, a journey toward the resurrected, living, glorified Jesus!

Grab your Bible and join me for the *Lent Scripture Journey.*

Alongside,

Keith

How to Use This Book

As I wrote the *Lent Scripture Journey* (and each of the Bible studies in the *Scripture Journey Series*), my goal was always to make this both easy-to-use and helpful for individuals, families, small groups or Sunday School classes.

For Individuals

Each day you will find guidance on what to read in your Bible. I don't print the actual passages in this book because part of going on a *Scripture Journey* is being in your Bible!

After the daily Bible reading, you will find a section called *For Reflection & Discussion*. In this section you will find questions, thoughts to ponder, or ideas for digging deeper.

Finally, at the end of each day I have a page for *Notes & Prayers*. Some Scripture journey-goers find this page helpful for jotting down ideas, thoughts, prayers, or even words or themes you want to explore more deeply after completing the *Lent Scripture Journey*. Others choose to use a separate journal or digital notebook (especially if you're reading the eBook rather than the physical book) for more thorough reflection, note-taking, or journaling.

One Recommendation: While using the *Lent Scripture Journey* as an individual is certainly beneficial, to get the most out of the journey – and have more fun doing it! – I highly recommend finding at least one friend to discuss what you are discovering.

For Families

I love doing *Scripture Journeys* with my wife and kids! Depending on the ages of your children you might need to adjust the *For Reflection & Discussion* section. Add some extra questions, leave some questions out, or put them in your own words. After all, you know your kids way better than I do!

While other *Scripture Journeys* can be done in 40 days, or extended to 8, 10, or even 12 weeks, the *Lent Scripture Journey* is a little different. Lent is a specific time period, so the 40 days will always begin on Ash Wednesday and conclude on Easter Sunday.

If your family is anything like mine, the idea that you will walk through the *Lent Scripture Journey* without ever missing a day is unrealistic or overwhelming. That's why I have made each day stand alone. Of course, you are welcome to double-up days and catch up. However, I have setup the *Lent Scripture Journey* by weeks and days (e.g. Week 3 – Wednesday) so you can simply look for the week and day corresponding to the day you're on and move forward. I have not put any dates on the *Lent Scripture Journey* so you can use it year after year!

Remember…This is *relational* time. It is not just about learning something or "getting through" the daily reading. God's desire – and design – is for us to be in relationship. Relationship with him. Relationship with each other.

For Small for Reflection & Discussions and Sunday School Classes

While some small group studies (or classes) are designed in a way that participants don't need to do much during the week, that is not the case for the *Lent Scripture Journey.* The discussion is only going to flow if participants are spending time "traveling alone" on the journey during week, and the small group or class time is a place for discussing what each person noticed on their journey.

Since the *For Reflection & Discussion* section is printed right in the book, there is no need for a "leader's guide" or "participant's guide." Each person has the same book. (I like simple!)

Week 1 – Ash Wednesday

Jesus is Coming!

Today's Passage: Luke 1:26-38

Did you notice the very first thing the angel said to Mary? After his greeting, he says, *"The Lord is with you."* The promise of Immanuel (Literally *"God with us"*) is given to Mary even before his birth. The promise of his current presence and his future presence.

The same promise is given to you today. The beautiful mystery is that as we journey toward Jesus – his life, his death, and his resurrection – he is present with us.

Let today, the first day of this journey, be a reminder that Jesus is here. He is with you. He is for you. He is the reason you can follow the angel's call... *"Do not be afraid."* And always remember this: The reason he came is not only so he could be Immanuel today, but also tomorrow, and for all eternity.

For Reflection & Discussion

- When do you sense Jesus's presence?
- Where do you need him to be present?
- Pray for Jesus to remind you of his presence. And offer him any fear you may be experiencing.

Notes & Prayers

Week 1 – Thursday

Jesus is Here!

Today's Passage: Luke 2:1-20

His life began so humbly. So strange for a king – The King – to have his first few hours of life be spent in a feeding trough. And yet, that's where we find Jesus.

We will end our journey praising the King for his defeat of death, his conquering of hell and the grave, and his triumphant exit from a dark tomb.

Today, praise him for his entry onto the scene. Praise him, as the shepherds did, for a discovery beyond comprehension. God put on flesh. The Creator became the created. The promised Immanuel became the in-the-flesh Immanuel. He came to Mary, Joseph, and even the shepherds. And he came to you.

For Reflection & Discussion

- Ponder the makes-no-sense humility of Jesus's birth.
- Let your mind wander through each scene. The birth. The heavenly concert. The shepherds finding Jesus. The rejoicing as they returned home.
- What makes you *"rejoice and praise God?"*

Notes & Prayers

Week 1 – Friday

Jesus is Presented, Dedicated, and Worshipped

Today's Passage: Luke 2:21-40

These verses contain the "common" and the "unbelievable." It was a common practice to dedicate a Jewish child at the age of eight days. It was very common to go to the temple and present your firstborn son to the Lord. It was even common to name a boy "Jesus."

But this common name, given by common parents, during a common dedication, was anything but common. For this 8-day-old child was the only person – before or since – who could actually *live out* the name he was given.

Jesus means *"Yahweh saves"* or *"The Lord is salvation."* Only *this* Jesus is the Yahweh who saves. Only he *is* salvation.

That's why Simeon and Anna had no choice but to worship him. Simeon praised the baby Jesus and proclaimed, *"I have seen your salvation."* Anna told everyone who would listen about this child – the source of redemption. May you worship and praise him as well.

For Reflection & Discussion

- Have you ever thought about the meaning of the name *Jesus*?

- Thank Jesus for your salvation and redemption.

- When have you seen the common and the unbelievable intersect in your own life?

Notes & Prayers

Week 1 – Saturday

Jesus Knows His Place

Today's Passage: Luke 2:41-52

Even at a young age, everything Jesus did was purposeful. He lived his whole life with intentional obedience. He was always, each minute of each day, with his Father and doing his Father's will.

As we journey toward Easter Morning, remember that everything he did was intentional. He knew where he was headed. He knew the parts that would be difficult. He knew the parts that would be fun. He knew the places he would go. He knew the faces he would see.

And he knew – and knows – your face. He knows your life. He knows your fun parts and difficult parts. He knows your needs. Your needs here on earth and your eternal needs.

Jesus continues to be in his Father's house. And he is smiling as he looks toward the day when he gets to say to you, *"Welcome home, my child. Welcome home."*

For Reflection & Discussion

- What would it have been like to realize that your child was lost for three days?

- Have you ever thought about the *intentionality* of Jesus? How does that inform your Bible reading?

- What can you do to live more intentionally in your Father's house (and his will)?

- Sometime today, imagine yourself entering heaven. And make sure you picture Jesus smiling...because he will be!

Notes & Prayers

WEEK 2 – MONDAY

JOHN BAPTIZES JESUS

Today's Passage: Matthew 3:13-17 (Also Mark 1:9-11, Luke 3:21-23 and John 1:29-34)

Yesterday we looked at the intentionality of Jesus. Today we get a picture of the Holy Spirit and God the Father.

Imagine the scene. Jesus comes to be baptized by his own cousin. John recognizes the seemingly backwards nature of what's taking place. After all, John has been baptizing people for the repentance of their sins. Jesus has never sinned and therefore, doesn't need to repent of anything. And yet, John agrees to be the baptizer, rather than the baptized.

As Jesus comes up out of the water, the Holy Spirit descends upon him. Baptism, for us, is certainly about repentance and forgiveness. But it is so much more! The Holy Spirit is present.

Then the Father speaks! Imagine that. Hearing the voice of the Father. His words are simple.

"This is my beloved son. With him I am well-pleased."

As you continue your journey through the life of Jesus, remember that each moment, each word, each encounter was empowered by the Holy Spirit and in accordance with the Father's will.

For Reflection & Discussion

- Imagine yourself as one of the people in the crowd. Imagine seeing the dove. Imagine hearing the Father's voice. Let yourself sit in awe.

- John went along with Jesus's request, even though it seemed backwards to him. Have you ever been obedient to a "backwards" call?

- When Jesus later speaks of people entering Heaven, he describes it as hearing *"Well done good and faithful servant! Share your master's joy."* Imagine the Father as "well-pleased" with you. Then make it your aim to live today *knowing* his joy and *increasing* his joy.

Notes & Prayers

Week 2 – Tuesday

Jesus is Tempted for 40 Days

Today's Passage: Luke 4:1-14 (Also Matthew 4:1-11 and Mark 1:12-13)

Today we find ourselves journeying through the wilderness with Jesus. Jesus spending 40 days in the wilderness is the backdrop for why there are 40 days of Lent. There is enough contained in these 14 verses to write an entire book. For today, let's look at what we can learn from the *order* of the events.

Many say that Jesus's earthly ministry began with his baptism. Today's reading shows us that is not the case. Yes, Jesus was filled with the Holy Spirit at his baptism (verse 1). But look at the last half of the verse...

> "...and he was led by the Spirit in the wilderness for forty days..."

He didn't begin his ministry. He went into the wilderness. Only after being tempted by the devil in the wilderness do we read verse 14...

"Then Jesus returned to Galilee in the power of the Spirit."

He was filled with the Spirit. He was led by the Spirit in the wilderness. He returned in the power of the Spirit.

If you and I want to be filled by the Spirit *and* walk in the power of the Spirit, I guess we better be willing to be led by the Spirit in the wilderness.

For Reflection & Discussion

- When have you sensed the Spirit's filling, presence, or power in your life?
- When have you walked *"in the wilderness?"* What was the outcome?
- Where do you need to invite, expect, and notice the Spirit's presence and power?

Notes & Prayers

Week 2 – Wednesday

John the Baptist Identifies Jesus As the Messiah

Today's Passage: John 1:19-34

As the journey continues, we find an unlikely "proclaimer" of Jesus. It's not an angel proclaiming Jesus as Messiah. It's not Simeon or Anna in the temple proclaiming that an 8-day-old baby is the Messiah. It's not the Spirit or the Father proclaiming that Jesus is the Messiah.

It is John. A 30-year-old man proclaiming that another 30-year-old man is the Messiah. Not only that, but it's his cousin! Oh...and he uses a very well-known passage of Scripture (from Isaiah 40) to let these religious leaders know that he – John the Baptist – is the one God had sent to prepare the way.

From then on, everyone – commoners and religious leaders alike – are on high alert. If the claim is false, it must be stopped. If the claim is true, it changes everything.

The same is true today. Which is why we're taking this journey through the whole life of Jesus. You need to look closely. After all, if Jesus really is the Messiah, it changes everything.

For Reflection & Discussion

- Have you ever proclaimed Jesus to people who didn't believe (or were anti-Jesus)?

- What makes you believe (or not believe) that Jesus is the Messiah?

- How would you answer someone who genuinely asks you why you believe what you believe about Jesus? Can you explain it?

Notes & Prayers

WEEK 2 – THURSDAY

JESUS REVEALS HIS PURPOSE

Today's Passage: Luke 4:14-21

Remember a couple days ago when Jesus was filled by the Spirit, led by the Spirit in the wilderness, and returned in the power of the Spirit? Today we pick up the story and look at what he did next.

Jesus began to teach, and Luke records the moment Jesus himself revealed his identity and his purpose. Everyone in the synagogue that day knew this particular passage in Isaiah 61 was speaking of the favorable year of the Lord.

For Jesus to say he is the fulfillment of this passage (verse 21) was to declare himself to be the Messiah. And what was his purpose? To preach good news. To release. To give sight. To set free. To proclaim the year of the Lord's favor.

The silence that day would have been deafening. No human can claim this about himself! Unless...just maybe...could it be true? Could Jesus really be the One?

For Reflection & Discussion

- When you think about Jesus, what are the elements of his "good news" that you are most grateful for today?
- Where do you need release, sight, freedom or favor?
- Pray about this for yourself…and someone else.

Notes & Prayers

Week 2 – Friday

Jesus Calls His First Disciples

Today's Passage: Luke 5:1-11 (Also Matthew 4:18-22 and Mark 1:16-20)

Today we see Jesus inviting others to join him on his journey. He begins by entering their world. He enters their boat. He teaches by their lake. He speaks to their neighbors.

Then he asks them to do something ridiculous. After all, they were the professional fisherman. He was a carpenter and traveling teacher. But oh, what a catch!

Then they do something ridiculous. They leave everything. They leave the known. They leave the comfortable. They leave because Jesus promises more. So much more.

In case you were wondering, he's calling you today. And he's calling you to so much more than you could ever imagine. Will you join him on the journey?

For Reflection & Discussion

- What does it mean to you that Jesus began by entering their world?

- What is the comfortable situation Jesus may be calling you to walk away from?

- Pray that Jesus would open your eyes to what he is calling you toward (as well as away from).

Notes & Prayers

WEEK 2 – SATURDAY

THE FIRST MIRACLE

Today's Passage: John 2:1-11

You might need to read that passage again. You might have missed one of the most important verses in the whole passage. After all, it's quite easy to miss.

There are a lot of amazing elements to this story. Jesus and his disciples at a big wedding. Jesus's mother is there as well. There is embarrassment and stress as they have run out of wine. There's a miracle. And not only a miracle, but Jesus's *first* miracle.

That's why Verse 9 is so easy to miss. And yet it's so important…

> "When the headwaiter tasted the water (after it had become wine), he did not know where it had come from – though the servants who had drawn the water knew."

Do you see it? Do you see whom Jesus let in on his very first miracle? Not the headwaiter. Not the families. Not the groom. Not even the bride!

The first people Jesus let in on the secret were the servants. The people nobody noticed. The people who, if they did their jobs correctly, were *supposed* to be unnoticed.

But not to Jesus. Jesus not only notices the unnoticed. He includes them. He celebrates them. He invites them to join him in his miracles. And he invites you as well.

For Reflection & Discussion

- How does Verse 9 change this passage for you?
- Have you ever felt unnoticed?
- Keep an eye out for someone you can notice, include, and celebrate today.

Notes & Prayers

Week 3 – Monday

Don't Get In the Way of Relationship

Today's Passage: John 2:13-25

If you have ever wondered what makes Jesus tick – and what ticks him off! – today's reading is where you will discover both.

What makes Jesus tick? *An intimate relationship between God and people.*

What ticks Jesus off? *Anyone getting in the way of that relationship.*

The money-changing and buying-and-selling had been transformed from an invitation to worship and build an intimate relationship with a Heavenly Father who rejoices over his people to a transactional barrier to that relationship.

And Jesus would have none of it! Do not get in the way of a relationship with the Father or you're going to have the wrath of the Son to deal with. And this was just the beginning.

Not even sin itself would get in the way. Jesus himself would clear the path. The cross and the empty tomb clear out the temple of our hearts. And intimacy is made possible once more.

For Reflection & Discussion

- When have you experienced intimacy with God?
- What needs to be "cleared out" so you can experience deeper intimacy?
- Have you ever seen the death and resurrection as the ultimate "clearing of the temple?"

Notes & Prayers

Week 3 – Tuesday

A Nighttime Conversation

Today's Passage: John 3:1-21

The most famous verse in the entire Bible (3:16) is found in today's reading. Reading it in the context of the conversation with Nicodemus sheds new light on this familiar verse.

First the *Who*: Nicodemus was a Pharisee. He supposedly knew what you needed to know to be in a relationship with God. He knew the Scriptures. He had faithfully served God for years. Maybe knowing the right information and doing the right things isn't enough.

Then the *When*: Notice that Nicodemus comes to Jesus at night. Why? Most likely, because Nicodemus knew that if anyone found out he went to Jesus, it would cost him. But he went. And Jesus didn't reprimand him for coming at night. Sometimes we go boldly. Sometimes we take a simple, tiny, tentative first step. The important thing is that you take your step – bold or timid – *toward* Jesus.

Finally, the *Why*: The Why is provided by Jesus himself. God sent. Jesus came. Because of love. In order to save. Not to condemn. (Read that last one again.) To bring light. To work in and through you. May you never read John 3:16 the same again.

For Reflection & Discussion

- What stood out to you from the context of reading the most famous Bible verse in context?

- Have you been tempted to put "knowing" and "doing" in place of being "in relationship with" Jesus?

- What is one step you can take toward Jesus this week?

- How can you remind yourself of Jesus's purpose to love and save – not condemn?

Notes & Prayers

Week 3 – Wednesday

A Forbidden Conversation

Today's Passage: John 4:4-42

Today's reading is one of the longest of our entire *Lent Scripture Journey*. But don't skim this reading. Soak in it. Maybe even read it two or three times. It's one of the most beautiful conversations in all of Scripture.

A woman so broken, so ashamed, she goes for water in the heat of the day. After all, that's the only time she won't encounter the judgmental glares of others. And yet, someone is there. A man. A Jewish man. Forbidden to speak with her, an unclean, Gentile woman.

However, instead of judgmental glares, Jesus offers gracious words. Instead of condemnation, Jesus offers an invitation. Instead of weighing her down with the sins of her past, he acknowledges them, and then calls her to a new future.

Today, may you see that Jesus's life, death, and resurrection as an ever-present reminder that he cares infinitely more about where you are headed than where you have been.

For Reflection & Discussion

- What is in your past that you have a hard time letting go of?

- How does Jesus's conversation with the woman at the well inform the way you view your own mistakes?

- What is the new future God is calling you to? (You might want to spend some time praying through this or talking with a friend about it.)

Notes & Prayers

Week 3 – Thursday

A Life Restored…With Authority

Today's Passage: Mark 1:21-28

Most people don't really like the word "authority." In only eight verses, we see this word twice today. Jesus teaches "*as one who had authority*" (Verse 22). Then he exercises authority over the demon. And then the people recognize that his teaching itself has authority (Verse 27).

Jesus has authority simply because of who he is. Jesus's teaching has authority because it comes from him.

We live in a world that claims that *we* are the ultimate authority. And yet, the person of Jesus, the acts of Jesus, and the teaching of Jesus say otherwise.

The beautiful thing is this: Submitting to the authority of who Jesus is and what he teaches doesn't hinder your life. Quite the opposite. Like the demon-possessed man, when Jesus exercises his authority in your life, you are set free!

For Reflection & Discussion

- What images and thoughts does the word "authority" conjure up in your mind?

- How does today's reading alter or expand that understanding?

- What "authority" are you trying to hold onto that you need to put under the authority of Jesus?

Notes & Prayers

Week 3 – Friday

Jesus...on Fasting

Today's Passage: Matthew 9:14-17 (Also Mark 2:18-22 and Luke 5:33-39)

Many people incorporate fasting into their celebration of Lent. Some people fast from something specific (like sugar, TV, social media, etc.). Others fast from eating one day each week. Still others fast for the full 40 days.

When Jesus speaks of fasting his focus is about the heart behind it. As always, Jesus is more concerned with why we are doing something than the specific detail of how we do it.

When questioned about why his disciples aren't fasting, he points to the relationship he has with them right now. (Notice he doesn't dismiss fasting altogether.) And in an earlier conversation on fasting (Matthew 6:16-18) he tells his disciples not to even let anyone know they are fasting.

Fasting has been, is now, and will always be about the relationship you have with your Heavenly Father *"who sees what is done in secret."* (Matthew 6:18)

For Reflection & Discussion

- Have you ever fasted? What was your focus...and experience?
- Talk to God about what you might fast from, and how it might deepen your relationship with him.

Notes & Prayers

Week 3 – Saturday

Resurrected and Returned to His Mother

Today's Passage: Luke 7:11-17

The end of our journey will find us at an empty tomb. Once dead...now alive.

Today we read of Jesus's first resurrection experience. (At least the first we have recorded in the Bible.) A dead boy. A grieving mother (and a widow as well). No husband. Now no son.

The grief is real. The grief is deep. Jesus approaches this heartbroken, sobbing widow, has compassion, and says two words...

"Don't weep."

If Jesus didn't know what was coming, this would be anything but compassion. Quite the opposite. It would be brutally unkind.

Only the One who holds the power of life and death in his hands can utter these words with compassion. Only the One who can speak life into a dead body can utter these words.

He speaks. And what was dead comes to life. He still speaks. And he still brings dead things to life.

For Reflection & Discussion

- Imagine the grief of the widow. Imagine hearing the words *"Don't weep."* Imagine seeing your dead son come to life! Sit in awe for a while.

- Have you ever witnessed the miraculous?

- What is something "dead" in your life that you need Jesus to "speak life" into? Spend some time praying through this.

Notes & Prayers

Week 4 – Monday

An Invitation to the Weary

Today's Passage: Matthew 11:25-30

Typically, the last three verses of today's reading are read on their own. *"Come to me…you who are weary…I will give you rest…my burden is light."*

The meaning doesn't necessarily "change" when we read them after reading what comes immediately before them, but it is deepened and enhanced. Jesus is praising his father for hiding some things from the *"wise and intelligent"* and revealing them to *"infants."*

He speaks of having all things entrusted to him by his Father. He speaks of the Son knowing the Father, and the Son revealing the Father to those he desires to.

Only then, does he call the weary and burdened to himself. The ones he is calling, the ones he is revealing the father to, the ones he is offering soul-rest to are the weary and burdened. Jesus knows that only when you admit your tiredness and weariness and offer him your burdens, can you ever truly understand what soul-rest looks like, not to mention the character of the One who offers it.

For Reflection & Discussion

- How difficult is it for you to admit when you are tired and weary?
- What burdens are you carrying that you need to offer to Jesus?
- When was the last time you felt truly, deeply, soulfully rested?

Notes & Prayers

Week 4 – Tuesday

What Type of Soil Are You?

Today's Passage: Mark 4:1-20 (Also Matthew 13:1-23 and Luke 8:1-15)

This is one of the most well-known, most written-about, and most preached-on of all Jesus's parables. The temptation is to read it without thinking about it. (If you just did that, you might want to take a few minutes to read it again more slowly.)

Understanding a parable and internalizing a parable are two very different things. Today, use this parable as a lens to evaluate your own receptiveness and openness to what God is trying to reveal to you and work inside you during this journey toward Easter.

Four types of soil. The hard path where nothing sticks. The rocky ground that doesn't allow any roots to grow. The thorny soil that hears and believes the Word, but allows the worries, deceitfulness, and desires of this world to choke it out. And finally, the good soil, that receives the Word, grows deep roots, and bears abundant fruit.

Sometimes, we look at one type of soil the way we look at the color of our eyes – one color for a lifetime. That's not how Jesus works. Soil can be tilled. Soil can be nourished. Soil can be broken up and cultivated. The path, the rocky soil, and the thorny soil can all *become* good soil.

For Reflection & Discussion

- What soil are you today?
- Which of the soils have you been?
- What have you done in the past (or could you do today) to cultivate yourself to be better, richer soil?

Notes & Prayers

Week 4 – Wednesday

Calm in the Midst of the Storm

Today's Passage: Mark 4:35-41 (Also Matthew 8:18-27, Luke 8:22-25 and John 6:16-21)

We find four questions in Mark's telling of this event. Two by the disciples and two by Jesus. All four hold a lesson for us.

"Teacher! Don't you care that we're going to die?"

This journey is taking us through the life of Jesus. On your own journey, as I'm sure you have experienced many times, storms will come. Some are mild and quickly pass. Others are shake-you-to-the-core storms. In those storms, the enemy loves to whisper this lie in your ear, *"Jesus doesn't even care."*

"Why are you afraid?"

Jesus calls you to examine your fears. What's the root cause? To answer the "Why" question, you have to look fear squarely between the eyes.

> "Do you still have no faith?"

This is the question that dives deep. The disciples had been with Jesus. They had seen him perform miracles. They had heard him teach. He knows that when our faith and trust in him grows, our fear has no choice to but fade.

> "Who then is this? Even the wind and the sea obey him!"

Mark says they were "*terrified*" when they said this. Matthew says, "*amazed*" and Luke says, "*fearful and amazed.*" This is a terrified awe that comes over them as they realize the power of Jesus, the Son of God. When you know God is in the storm with you, your awe shifts away from the original fear and leads to the worship of the One who is much, much bigger than any storm.

For Reflection & Discussion

- What is your "storm?"
- When have you seen God pull you through a storm and into peace?
- Have you ever been "fearful and amazed" as you think about and experience the power of God?

Notes & Prayers

Week 4 – Thursday

A Healing...in the Midst of Busyness

Today's Passage: Mark 5:24-34 (Also Matthew 9:20-22 and Luke 8:42-48)

As Jesus was walking along the way, he teaches us a lesson on busyness. People have said forever, *"Don't sacrifice the important for the urgent."* But what if we're busy with things that are important?

After all, the context for today's reading is Jesus on his way to raise a young girl from the dead. It doesn't get more important than that!

One woman, of the many people pressing in on him, touches him, and he senses the power go out from him. Someone touched him. Someone was healed.

He stopped everything and engaged. He sought her out. He spoke with her. He healed her. He saved her.

Today, Jesus is still busy with many important things. And yet, today, he is seeking you out. He is speaking to you. He is ready to touch you, heal you, and save you.

For Reflection & Discussion

- Do you have trouble slowing down and taking time for others?

- Do you have trouble slowing down and spending time with Jesus?

- Is there an area of your life you desperately need Jesus to touch and heal?

Notes & Prayers

Week 4 – Friday

What Will You Offer?

Today's Passage: John 6:1-15 (Also Matthew 14:13-21, Mark 6:30-44 and Luke 9:10-17)

Many parts of the journey toward the empty tomb are hard. Death. Suffering. Wilderness. Fasting. Storms.

Today we see Jesus having fun. I can't read today's passage without picturing Jesus smiling. Smiling when he's asking Philip what he should do (even when he already knows what he's going to do). Smiling when Andrew brings the boy with a sack lunch (even though Andrew doesn't see what good it's going to do). Smiling as he takes the sack lunch from the boy. (The text doesn't say it, but I'm pretty sure Jesus winked at the kid.) Smiling as more than 5,000 people ate... and ate...and ate. Smiling as the leftovers filled twelve baskets.

Yes. Today I think Jesus had fun. I also think he still likes to have fun. He enjoys taking what little we offer – in generous faith – and multiplying it to serve more people than we could ever dream.

For Reflection & Discussion

- Have you ever hesitated to offer something to God because you simply didn't think it was "big enough" or "good enough?"

- Have you ever experienced God multiply a seemingly small offering into something more?

- Have you ever pictured Jesus having fun as he performed a miracle? If not, how does that change your perception of Jesus?

Notes & Prayers

Week 4 – Saturday

Jesus Knows What's Coming

Today's Passage: Mark 8:31-9:1 (Also Matthew 16:21-28 and Luke 9:21-27)

It is one thing to endure suffering. It is another to know you are going to suffer and still walk toward it. Jesus knows what's coming. Most likely, he is not too many weeks or months from entering Jerusalem…and the worst several days of his life.

He speaks of suffering. He speaks of being rejected. He speaks of being killed. And yes, he speaks of rising from the dead.

Apparently, Peter didn't hear – or understand – the part about rising from the dead. He was fixated on the suffering, rejection, and killing. So, instead of offering Jesus compassion, or simply listening, he pulls Jesus aside and rebukes him.

Jesus's response? To turn the conversation around and rebuke Peter for not focusing on God's concerns but his own. Then he takes it a step further and calls each person to take up their own cross and follow. Then he takes it yet another step further and calls each of us to lay down our very lives.

Will you walk toward his call or ignore it?

For Reflection & Discussion

- Have you ever had a hard circumstance you knew would be hard *and* you knew was God's will? What was your response?
- What might "carrying your own cross" look like for you?
- Have you ever been tempted to be ashamed of Jesus?

Notes & Prayers

Week 5 – Monday

A Call to Fully Commit

Today's Passage: Luke 9:57-62 (Also Matthew 8:19-22)

This one is hard. (Warning: The days ahead are not going to get easier. This is oftentimes a rough journey.)

This one is hard because it's a gut-check. Like the people in this passage, we say, *"Jesus, we'll follow you. Anywhere. Just say the word and I'll go."*

The problem with saying we'll follow Jesus, is that Jesus always – every time – says, *"Outstanding! Follow me."*

The challenge is that "following" looks different for each of us. Sometimes following looks a lot like staying and deeply investing where he has us. Other times following looks like a great adventure. Still other times following looks like a costly-and-not-very-fun journey.

Unfortunately, it's just as easy to make excuses for *not* following Jesus as it is to tell him you will follow him in the first place. *But first... Right after I...*

There will always be a good reason (in our own minds) to follow Jesus a little later. And yet, his call is to follow him…fully…right now.

For Reflection & Discussion

- Is there anything God is asking you to do that you're hesitating on? Why is that?
- What is God asking you to do right now? (Spend some time praying and/or journaling about this one.)
- Have you ever followed God wholeheartedly? What was the outcome?

Notes & Prayers

Week 5 – Tuesday

The Right Time

Today's Passage: John 7:1-13

It is heartbreaking when people don't believe in you. It is even more heartbreaking when their unbelief turns into mocking. And it is truly devastating when the unbelief and mocking comes from your family.

That was the case with Jesus's brothers. The Festival of Shelters is near. The brothers sarcastically mock Jesus as one who is seeking public recognition.

In the midst of enduring the mocking – and surely experiencing sadness over his brothers' unbelief – Jesus knows his call. He knows his timing. He knows what he has to do. And he sticks to it.

It couldn't have been easy. The right thing rarely is.

For Reflection & Discussion

- Have you ever been disbelieved or mocked? How did you handle it?

- Have you ever been so sure of God's calling that you were willing to endure hardship (internally or externally) to be obedient?

- Is there any relationship that is hard now that you would like to see restored? (After all, scholars believe that the Bible books of *James* and *Jude* were written by two of Jesus's previously unbelieving brothers!)

Notes & Prayers

Week 5 – Wednesday

Forgiveness...and a Call to More

Today's Passage: John 8:2-11

Many times, the focus of this passage is about Jesus saying, *"The one without sin among you should be the first to throw a stone at her."* Certainly an important message. But in light of the journey we are one, let's focus on the conversation he has with the woman herself.

First, Jesus stands up for her. When others condemn, he takes the focus off of her and onto himself. When others walk away, he stays.

Second, Jesus doesn't condemn. Others do. Jesus does not. Jesus forgives.

Third, Jesus calls her to sin no more. He calls her to a better life than she would ever call herself to.

Hmmm...taking the focus off our sin and onto himself. Forgiving when he could have condemned. Calling us to more than we would ever call ourselves to. Sounds a lot like what happened with the cross and the empty tomb, wouldn't you say?

For Reflection & Discussion

- Have you ever felt judged or condemned? How did you react?

- Have you ever been the one to judge or condemn? Do you need to ask for forgiveness?

- Spend some time thanking Jesus for taking your sin and shame, forgiving instead of condemning, and calling you to a much better life than you would ever have on your own.

Notes & Prayers

Week 5 – Thursday

The Shepherd Every Sheep Needs

Today's Passage: John 10:1-18

Sheep don't know everything the shepherd is going to do. But they know the shepherd. They trust the shepherd. They follow the shepherd. They listen for the shepherd's voice.

As the final trip to Jerusalem draws ever closer, Jesus uses the analogy of the sheep and shepherd to help them understand his relationship with us a little better.

The Good Shepherd enters the sheep pen. He goes to where the sheep are. Jesus is meeting you where you are.

The Good Shepherd offers his sheep life to the full. The life of the sheep is better because the Good Shepherd makes it so. Jesus offers you life to the full as well.

The Good Shepherd knows the sheep. Since the earliest days, it has always been about the relationship. You are fully known. And you are fully loved.

The Good Shepherd lays down his life for the sheep (and takes it up again). Jesus is being very intentional. Jesus knows what he's saying. Jesus knows what's coming. After all, he's the Good Shepherd.

For Reflection & Discussion

- How does it feel to know that Jesus, the Good Shepherd, pursues you and comes to your "sheep pen?"
- Thank Jesus for his offer of "*life to the full.*"
- What does it mean to you that you are fully known and fully loved?

Notes & Prayers

Week 5 – Friday

Only the Sign of Jonah.

Today's Passage: Matthew 12:38-42 (Also Luke 11:29-36)

Signs and wonders. We all think that "if we could just see" then we would believe. But that's never been the case. From the earliest pages of the Bible all the way through today, people have seen plenty. And yet, our unbelief persists.

On the pages of Scripture, we read of audible words from God, burning bushes, miracles, healing, teaching, lame people dancing, blind people seeing, dead people…well…living!

Doubt will always find a way to keep us in our unbelief. Jesus knew it. That's why, when asked for "just one more sign," he pointed toward the empty tomb. Jonah was in the fish for three days. Jesus would be in the tomb for three days.

Then he would rise. He would walk out of the tomb. After all, if saying you are going to die and rise after three days – and then actually doing it! – isn't enough, nothing will be.

For Reflection & Discussion

- How have you played the "just one more sign" game with God?

- What led you to put your faith in Jesus? A miracle? A conversation? A relationship?

- What doubts do you need to bring to Jesus? (He can handle your authentic questions.)

Notes & Prayers

WEEK 5 – SATURDAY

JESUS WIL RETURN...AND HE KNOWS IT

Today's Passage: Matthew 25:1-13 (Also Mark 13:32-37 and Luke 12:35-48)

Jesus has spoken of his suffering. He has pointed to his death. He has clearly told them that he would rise again.

In today's reading, Jesus points to his ultimate return. Jesus always knew the endgame wasn't just conquering sin (although that's pretty amazing). It wasn't even conquering death. It was relationship. (Check out the book of *Revelation* if you want the full picture.)

As he thinks about this ultimate return, Jesus points out even *he* doesn't know the day or hour. And if Jesus doesn't know, then why would we ever be arrogant enough to think we can figure it out.

It's not about knowing *when* it is going to happen. It is about living a *prepared life*. Being wise. Being alert. Being obedient. Being ready.

For Reflection & Discussion

- What does it mean to you that, even as he prepared for his crucifixion and resurrection, Jesus was keeping his *ultimate return* in mind?

- Thank Jesus for all that he has done to make an eternal relationship with you possible.

- How might you live more alert, more prepared, more ready?

Notes & Prayers

Week 6 – Monday

Jesus is Warned…and Still Presses On

Today's Passage: Luke 13:31-33

Some would call it "crazy." Others would say "determined." Jesus is warned that Herod wants him dead. The people telling him this (the Pharisees) also want him dead.

Jesus's response? *"I'm going anyway."* (That's the Keith Ferrin Paraphrase.)

How could he do it? How could he walk directly into danger? Especially when he had already pointed out that betrayal, mocking, beating, and killing was in his future.

The hint is the final phrase of Verse 32…

"…on the third day I will complete my work."

Remember, his whole life and ministry has been a tunnel vision focus on making a way for the Father, Son, Holy Spirit – and you! – to live together for all eternity.

The death and resurrection of Jesus *complete* that work. If he quit now, he wouldn't have completed the necessary work for you to live forever with him. And that was something he simply could not accept.

For Reflection & Discussions

- Is there anything you are so called to and driven toward that you would endure suffering to achieve it?
- How does Jesus's response to the warning challenge and encourage you?
- How does it make you feel that spending eternity with you is what drove Jesus to endure what he went through?

Notes & Prayers

Week 6 – Tuesday

Jesus Answers…Weeps…and Resurrects!

Today's Passage: John 11:1-44

Back in Week 3, we looked at Jesus's first resurrection (of the little boy). Today we look at his most famous resurrection (other than his own of course).

Lazarus, Martha, and Mary. Friends. People he knew and loved. And now Lazarus is dead…and has been for several days.

Jesus heads into Bethany, has a conversation with disappointed and confused Martha, and then another with heartbroken and weeping Mary.

With Martha, he answers her questions. With Mary, he weeps with her.

Now remember, Jesus knows that Lazarus's visit to the tomb is temporary. He knows he is only minutes away from watching Lazarus walk out of the tomb.

Still...he weeps.

The lesson is clear. Future healing and resurrection do not dismiss the reality of present questions and heartache. You can place confident hope in the empty tomb and eternity *and* bring your questions and sorrow to Jesus. And he will meet you there.

For Reflection & Discussion

- What do you think it was like – knowing what was in store for him – for Jesus to experience the death and resurrection of others.
- What does it mean to you that Jesus answered Martha's questions?
- What does it mean to you that Jesus wept with Mary?
- What struggle or sorrow have you been keeping buried because you thought Jesus couldn't handle it?

Notes & Prayers

Week 6 – Wednesday

The Plot and the Prediction

Today's Passage: John 11:45-54

We have seen the religious leaders butting heads with Jesus for quite a while. Today's reading is the clearest picture of the actual plot against him. People who saw what Jesus did (raise Lazarus) either believed…or told the religious leaders. Imagine witnessing a resurrection – after four days in a tomb! – and still not believing.

The chief priests and Pharisees are at a loss. They recognize that Jesus is doing miraculous signs. The also realize that if he keeps going, they will be in trouble with the Romans.

Then Caiaphas, the high priest, speaks. His words leave nothing unclear. Jesus must die. It is good for the leaders in the room. And it is good for the entire Jewish nation.

Notice the first words of Verse 51…

> "He did not say this on his own…"

He was speaking of something God the Father knew would come to pass. The Holy Spirit also knew. Jesus himself knew. In fact, only one chapter earlier, Jesus spoke of his death when he said, *"No one takes it [my life] from me, but I lay it down on my own."* (John 10:18)

Yes...they are plotting. Yes...Caiaphas is prophesying. But don't ever forget that when it comes to Jesus laying down his life for you, this was what God planned all along.

For Reflection & Discussion

- Some people saw Lazarus resurrected and believed. What led to your belief?
- How different is it that Jesus offered his life, rather than having it taken from him?
- How have you seen God use the acts of sinful people for his greater purposes?

Notes & Prayers

Week 6 – Thursday

They Don't Understand

Today's Passage: Luke 18:31-34 (Also Matthew 20:17-19 and Mark 10:32-34)

With our knowledge of the full story of Jesus, this passage is difficult to comprehend. After all, what is there not to understand?

Jesus tells them they're going to Jerusalem. He tells them the prophet's words will come true. (These were Jewish men. They knew the Scriptures.) He tells them he's going to be handed over. He tells them he will be mocked, insulted, spit on, flogged, and killed. He tells them he will rise.

Luke includes an extra verse Matthew and Mark omit. Two sentences.

> "They understood none of these things. The meaning of the saying was hidden from them, and they did not grasp what was said."

The concept of Jesus, the Messiah, *not* taking his rightful place of leadership was absolutely unfathomable. Beyond anything they could wrap their brains around. Jesus was crystal clear. And yet, they had "*no grasp*" of what he was saying.

So often, we do the same thing today. The Holy Spirit is speaking to our hearts, guiding us through circumstances, and even leading us through the words of trusted friends. But we are so certain of what God is going to do – and how he will do it – we have no grasp of what he is doing.

For Reflection & Discussion

- Have you ever felt confused by what God was doing?

- Have you ever looked back at your life many months or years and been amazed at how you could have missed what God was doing or saying?

- How do you think Jesus felt as his best friends had no grasp of what he was saying?

Notes & Prayers

Week 6 – Friday

Real Power and Leadership

Today's Passage: Matthew 20:20-28 (Also Mark 10:35-45)

Matthew and Mark both record the conversation immediately following yesterday's the-disciples-had-no-grasp conversation. Apparently, the mother of James and John is traveling with them. She approaches Jesus and asks that her sons get the two highest positions of power in Jesus's kingdom (sitting at his right and left hand). Mark says that James and John are the ones who asked Jesus directly. Either way, it's a bold question for sure!

In the previous conversation, the disciples can't understand what Jesus was saying. In this conversation, Jesus says they don't understand what they are asking.

They want power and leadership. They just don't want it to cost them anything. They want it handed to them. They fail to understand that power and leadership are costly.

And then he contrasts worldly power with godly power. Worldly power demands honor and respect. Godly power gives honor and respect. Worldly power demands others serve you. Godly power seeks out ways to serve.

I wonder how many times James and John thought about this conversation over the days and weeks between now and seeing the resurrected, glorified Jesus.

For Reflection & Discussion

- When have you experienced worldly power and leadership?
- When have you experienced godly power and leadership?
- Where and how is God calling you to serve those around you?

Notes & Prayers

WEEK 6 – SATURDAY

WHAT SALVATION LOOKS LIKE IN REAL LIFE

Today's Passage: Luke 19:1-10

Jesus was fewer than 20 miles from Jerusalem. Only days before he rides into Jerusalem on a donkey's colt. The weight of what is to come must be getting heavier.

As he enters Jericho, the crowds surround him. Unfortunately, Zacchaeus can't see Jesus. The Bible tells us it was because he was short. I wonder if he also climbs the tree to see Jesus from a place where he can avoid the stares and jeers of people who despise this hated tax collector.

Imagine everyone's surprise – including Zacchaeus's – when Jesus stops, looks up, speaks to Zacchaeus, and tells him *"...it is necessary for me to stay at your house."*

What?! Stay at his house? They are almost to Jerusalem. Jesus is going to spend one of his final nights outside the city with this...this...*tax collector?* Well...yes. Yes, he is.

Zacchaeus climbed down, welcomed Jesus into his home, and was never the same. Jesus is only days away from dying for the salvation of the world. But on this day, we see salvation in real life. We see a man transformed. We see a selfish sinner become a generous disciple. Praise Jesus!

For Reflection & Discussion

- Have you ever judged someone Jesus would want you to love?
- To what lengths will you go to get closer to Jesus?
- In what ways have you been transformed by the person and presence of Jesus?

Notes & Prayers

Week 7 – Monday

An Unlikely Anointing

Today's Passage: John 12:1-11 (Also Matthew 26:6-13 and Mark 14:3-9)

Allow yourself to enter this scene. This is the day before the triumphal entry. Jesus and his disciples are at the home Simon the leper (according to Matthew and Mark), but Martha, Mary, and Lazarus – now alive and healthy – are there as well. Disciples are confused. Judas Iscariot is about to betray the Messiah.

Wait! What's that aroma? Perfume. Expensive perfume. And it's on Jesus's feet! This is crazy.

People start grumbling. Judas actually speaks up. *"What are you doing? This is a waste! We could have at least sold the perfume and given it to the poor."*

As always, Jesus knew the heart. He knew Judas's heart. And he knew Mary's heart. He also knew something no one else knew, or at least no one else understood. This was a burial anointing. He was about to die.

Yes. Jesus knew Judas's heart and Mary's heart. Jesus also knows your heart. By now we know that Jesus had set his own heart toward Jerusalem. But that's a story for tomorrow...

For Reflection & Discussion

- Imagine the myriad of emotions in the room. Jesus's. Mary's. The disciples. Judas's. The people at the dinner. Some were heavy. And some were clueless. Allow yourself to sit with whatever emotions you have today as you ponder the anointing of Jesus.

- Have you ever done anything "extravagant" in an effort to serve or honor Jesus?

- Is it more comforting or concerning that Jesus fully knows your heart?

Notes & Prayers

WEEK 7 – TUESDAY

HOSANNA! JESUS ENTERS THE CITY

Today's Passage: Matthew 21:1-11 (Also Mark 11:1-11, Luke 19:28-44 and John 12:12-19)

This event is recorded in all four gospels. You might want to take some time and read each account today. Notice the different details each gospel writer includes. And notice the detail they all include...

The crowd worships with shouts of, *"Hosanna!"* Hosanna is a word that is both a *crying out* for one to save us and a *worshipping* of the One who saves.

This week is going to be hard. It was hard for Jesus. If we enter into the story, it will be hard for us. But not today.

Today is about worship. Today is about *"Hosanna!"* Today is about proclaiming that Jesus is the only One who saves. Today is about crying out for him to save us. Today is about hands lifted high. Today is about palms on the ground.

Today is a day to worship. Enjoy it!

For Reflection & Discussion

- How do you worship? Singing? Silence? Walking in nature? Dancing?
- What do you think it was like for Jesus to hear the shouts and praises of the crowd, knowing what was coming?
- What part of your life needs to shout *"Hosanna!"*?

Notes & Prayers

Week 7 – Wednesday

Never Enough for Everyone

Today's Passage: John 12:37-50

Jesus has performed miracles. He has taught. He has raised the dead. He has healed the sick. He has shown compassion. He has confronted the religious leaders. He has cleared the temple. He has journeyed toward this moment, this Holy Week, for three years.

And yet, many still didn't believe. And many who did believe didn't profess their belief because they were afraid.

Sounds like today, don't you think?

God has revealed himself in so many ways. And yet, there are many who don't believe. Jesus knew there would always be people who wouldn't believe, no matter how much "evidence" they are shown. And he still did and spoke exactly what the Father told him. Maybe you and I should do the same.

For Reflection & Discussion

- Do you get frustrated when people don't believe?

- Do you trust that the Holy Spirit is better at preparing hearts and drawing people to the Father than you are?

- Is there anyone God is asking you to share his love with...even if they won't believe and receive it?

Notes & Prayers

Week 7 – Thursday

The Betrayed Servant

Today's Passage: John 13:1-20

It's the day before the darkest day in history. Jesus knows what's coming. Jesus is having one last meal with his disciples. This is it. The last time all 13 of them will be together. One is about to betray him. One is about to deny him – three times. The rest are all about to scatter.

And what does Jesus do? He serves them. He removes his outer garment, fills a bowl with water, grabs a towel, and starts washing feet. The feet of the one who will deny him. The feet of the ones who will scatter. And yes, even the feet of the one who will betray him.

The humble servanthood of Jesus is nothing short of awe-inspiring.

For Reflection & Discussion

- Have you ever served others when it was hard? What was the result?
- How does Jesus's servanthood challenge, encourage, or inspire you?
- Spend some time praying for those it's difficult for you to serve.

Notes & Prayers

WEEK 7 – FRIDAY

THE WORST, BEST FRIDAY.

Today's Passage: Matthew 27:1-56 (Also Mark 15:1-41, Luke 22:66-23:49 and John 18:28-19:42)

We call this day Good Friday. Not because it was good, but because what was accomplished was good. The day itself was the darkest day the world has ever known.

As you read, go slowly. Allow this familiar story to wash over you with fresh emotions. Allow each mocking word to fill your ears. Allow each unjust accusation to make you angry. Allow each violent blow to bruise your soul. Allow the crown of thorns to make you wince. Allow the nails to pierce your heart.

And then hear the words of your Lord, *"It is finished."* And remember, he was thinking of you when he said them. Your sin has been dealt with. Forever.

Yes indeed. This was the worst, best Friday in history.

For Reflection & Discussion

- What stood out to you as you read these events with new eyes?
- How does the suffering of Jesus make you feel?
- What do the words *"It is finished."* mean to you?

Notes & Prayers

Week 7 – Saturday

The Most Confusing Day in History

Today's Passage: Luke 23:56b

Half of one verse. That's it. Other than the few verses devoted to a conversation between the chief priests, Pharisees, and Pilate about guarding the tomb, one half of one verse is all we have in the Bible about that Saturday.

> "And they rested on the Sabbath according to the commandment."

That's it. Nothing else is written about that day. The most confusing day in history.

Jesus is dead. But he was the One. He was the Messiah. At least they thought so. And now? He was dead. Buried in a borrowed tomb.

There was nothing to do. Except go home. And weep.

For Reflection & Discussion

- Sit in the confusion today. Don't move through it too quickly.
- When have you been confused or broken about what God is doing – or not doing?

Notes & Prayers

Easter Sunday

Risen! He is alive!

Today's Passage: John 20 (Also Matthew 28, Mark 16:1-13 and Luke 24:1-12)

Our *Lent Scripture Journey* has brought us to this day. Our journey has taken us right here. To an empty tomb. To a stone that has been rolled away.

He is not here. He has risen.

Death is defeated. Sin is no longer your identity. Separation is no longer your destiny.

Jesus has dealt with sin and conquered death. He is alive!

May your endless, eternal journey with your risen Savior be a journey you rejoice in taking each and every moment of each and every day.

Happy Easter! He has risen...indeed!

About the Author

Am I the only one who thinks it is a little bit strange that the "About the Author" page is typically the only page in an entire book written in the third person? After all, I am the author. I am writing this page. It feels a bit weird to write about myself in the third person.

So let's try this...

I, Keith Ferrin, am an author, speaker, storyteller, and messaging coach. My passion is helping individuals, families, and entire church communities move from "should" to "want" when it comes to reading the Bible. I believe the Bible isn't just true, but it's also awesome! When I'm not the one on stage, I'm typically helping coach the people who are. I love to help C-level leaders, teams, pastors and entrepreneurs simplify their messages and deliver them well.

Actually, I guess all that is more of what I "do." As far as who I am...I am a disciple of Jesus Christ, a husband to Kari (world's most outstanding wife), and a father to Sarah, Caleb, and Hannah (the three coolest – and craziest – kids on the planet).

In case you are still reading…I am also a coffee drinker, ice cream eater, amateur guitar player, lover of twisty-turny movies, and eater of almost any kind of food (except olives).

If you're looking for me, head on up to Seattle. I will be the happy guy hanging out with his wife and kids doing something outside. Unless, of course, it is family movie night. Then we'll be inside.

A Few of My Other Books

Ephesians Scripture Journey

When it comes to living out our faith, the temptation is to make it all about morality – doing the "right" things and avoiding the "wrong" things. In Paul's letter to the *Ephesians*, he takes a different approach altogether. With guidance for individuals, families and small groups, the 40-Day *Ephesians Scripture Journey* will remind you of your identity in Christ, so you can live with greater freedom, boldness, authenticity, and purpose. Read Reviews on Amazon

How to Enjoy Reading Your Bible

Do you enjoy the Bible? If we enjoy the Bible, we will read it. If we enjoy it, we'll talk about it. If we enjoy it, consistency won't be a problem. After almost three decades of speaking and writing, I have compiled my "Top 10 Tips" for enjoying the Bible. Tips that are applicable immediately. Written using stories, analogies, and common language, these tips are equally accessible for someone who is exploring, is new to faith in Jesus, or has been hanging out with Jesus for decades. If you want to enjoy the Bible – I wrote this book for you. Because believing it's true is not enough. Read Reviews on Amazon

Like Ice Cream: The Scoop on Helping the Next Generation Fall in Love with God's Word

What if passing on a love for God's Word could be as natural – and enjoyable – as passing on a love for ice cream? I believe it can be. When it comes to helping the next generation fall in love with the Bible, the principles are surprisingly similar to the way a love for ice cream gets passed on from generation to generation. Whether you are a parent, grandparent, youth pastor – or anyone who cares deeply about the next generation – you will find *Like Ice Cream* filled with encouragement and practical ideas you can start using today. Read Reviews on Amazon

Falling in Love with God's Word

This book will help you discover what God always intended Bible study to be. God wants you to understand His Word. He wants you to enjoy your time in His Word. He wants you to remember what you read in His Word. In this book, I walk you through my entire process for deeply studying a book of the Bible. My prayer is this book will transform your Bible study time in a way that will allow God to use His Word to transform you! Read Reviews on Amazon

Rapid Bible Read Thru

Have you ever read through the whole Bible? Have you ever started…only to stop after a few weeks? Do you wish you understood the Bible better? Do you long to know The Author more deeply? If so, *Rapid Bible Read Thru* is just what you need!

Is it a challenge? *Yes*. It is easier than most people think? *Absolutely*. Will it transform your understanding of the Bible and deeper your relationship with God? *No doubt!* This book will walk you step-by-step through the Why, What, and How of doing a *Rapid Bible Read Thru*. Read Reviews on Amazon

Bible Praying for Parents

As parents, we want to pray for our kids. We know we should pray for them. And yet, our prayers often feel repetitive. So then, how do we know what to pray? How do we know we are covering every aspect of their lives (rather than only what's urgent at the moment)? The answer is *Bible Praying*. After all, when we pray God's Word, we pray God's will.

I wrote this book with my friend Judy Fetzer, who introduced me to praying the words of Scripture for our children. In this book we've turned 365 Bible passages (in 20+ categories) into prayer. We've also included a section of *Bible Blessings* straight from God's Word. Read Reviews on Amazon

Let's Connect!

I love to connect with my readers. Truly. Shoot me an email. I'll write back.

There are lots of ways we can connect. Here are a couple:

- Email: keith@keithferrin.com
- Blog: www.keithferrin.com

Social Media (You can find me using @KeithFerrin pretty much anywhere.)

Instagram • Facebook • YouTube • LinkedIn • Pinterest • Twitter

If you have a question, comment, or idea for another book, please shoot me a note. I'd love to hear from you.

Alongside,

Made in United States
Troutdale, OR
03/15/2025